AM.

© The Wordsworth Trust, Dove Cottage,
Grasmere, Cumbria LA22 9SH, 2007
Poems © Neil Rollinson
All rights reserved

Designed by Craig Birtles

ISBN 978 1 905256 27 3

Printed by Titus Wilson, Kendal

AMPHIBIANS

Neil Rollinson

For the lovely Bernie after our dirty weekend in Limerick —

thanks for the hot snogs X

Neil

THE WORDSWORTH TRUST

Acknowledgements

Thanks are due to the Wordsworth Trust, especially to David Wilson for his friendship and support, and to Pamela Woof, who continues to be an inspiration to us all. Craig for his brilliant design and indefatigable good humour, and a big thanks to Mark for keeping me sane among all the madness. To Rich for getting me to Grasmere in the first place, and to the whole posse who live and work at Town End: you know who you are. A big thanks to all the nutcases in Tweedies who made life endurable during the dark, wet winters (take the bloody nozzles of the pumps!).

Some of these poems were first published in my recent collection of poems entitled *Demolition*, published by Jonathan Cape (2007) 'Tornado,' 'The Path of a Thousand Hellos,' and 'GPS.' A special thanks to them, and to my editor Robin Robertson.

for Rich

Contents

Amphibians	1
The Path of a Thousand Hellos	2
Feathers	4
Grasmere 5 A.M	5
GPS	8
Arrival	10
Ancestors	11
Frog March	12
Fledgling	14
Still-life with Cricketers	15
Mean	16
Reply	18
Grizedale Tarn	19
Tornado	20
The Bus	21

Amphibians

It rained for a month, a downpour
that never stopped, the lanes turned to rivers,
the lake rose and quivered on the lip
of the road like a lid of mercury holding the water in.
The gutters rang, the culverts gulped,
we forgot what the blue sky looked like,
we braved the pavements with our shopping bags,
like the first amphibians, unused to such an element.
At night we'd sleep to the constant drumming
and dream we could breathe under water,
the house grew damp, our books swelled
in their cases, light bulbs hissed in their sockets,
and our coats dripped in the hallway.
We grew depressed and hardly spoke, except
in gurgles and burps, the submarine lingo
of pond-life, croaking like toads in a swamp.
We sat by our fires and waited, reading the wind
for a sign, for a hint of a change in the weather.
It would have to stop soon, that's all we believed,
it couldn't keep raining forever.

The Path of a Thousand Hellos

'When all at once I saw a crowd'

It begins at the garden gate; by the time
you reach How Top you've greeted seven,
more by the pond and four by the stile,
their jolly rounded vowels mingling
with brook and crow, a thousand blended notes:
hello, hello. By White Moss Common
there're sixteen more: *good morning, hi,*
that mindless ramblers' bonhomie, as if,
because we're out here, all together,
we ought to greet each other, heartily.

Give me Regent Street on Monday morning,
that sense of solitude you find in the city.
I can walk the mile of Oxford Street in perfect anonymity,
or stroll from Clerkenwell to Notting Hill
and never greet a soul though thousands pass,
it's like a journey through wastelands full of ghosts;
but this is hell, hailing everyone you meet,
the vapid smiles, the grins, the beaming faces.

At Rydal Mount there's half a coachful,
brimming with the bliss of Lakeland, poetry,
the romance of it all. *Hello, what a beautiful day.*
Like fuck it is, you want to say, but don't.

I leave the track and head up over Heron Pike,
the long, steep slog to Fairfield, where I know
that few, if any, will have ventured: the gnarled
and wizened, the grumpy or the antisocial;
this is where I like it, in the vicious gale, where words
get blown away before they're ever heard,
and a simple nod will do, to recognise a kindred soul,
out seeking solitude among the hills.

Feathers

A cold winter's evening between trains
and the air is full of feathers, swirling
in the station lights like a flurry of snow;
a man laid out on the cold stone,
two figures knelt over him, in prayer,
a defibrillator lies at his side like a bible.
Stand back. It warns in its automated voice.
It beeps, then: bang! The shock goes through him,
shaking his boots, blowing the down from his coat.
He sleeps on. They give him another shot,
so strong he almost sits up, but then settles again
on the platform edge, so tired he will not wake.
A crowd has gathered round to see
what suffering looks like. It's been a long day,
but we stay to watch, in the hope he'll rise,
full of electric, his hair standing on end,
but none the worse for that. They try again.
His body quakes under the current, feathers
pour out of him like light, like a pillow fight.
You can see the resignation on the faces
of the medics, their body language. They whisper
to each other through the blizzard, lay the box
on his chest and carry him off, through all
the mute witnesses. Platform 2, Oxenholme,
between trains, the air is full of feathers
swirling in the dark like a flurry of snow.

Grasmere 5 AM

for C.B

The light, the light, she says
running into the dawn,
the air full of rain and birdsong.
I stumble out of the dark house,
the smoke and music, into a green world.
It's the Dawn of the Dead,
people are stumbling about, hand in hand,
smoking, or drinking from bottles,
kissing in the limpid, wet dawn.

I blow a ring of blue smoke
and watch it disappear, like a halo
over my head. Water falls off the fells
in white ribbons.

Joe with his flaming red hair
is pounding sound across Town End.
You can feel the bass in the soles of your feet.
It makes this place seem better
than it ever did; the light and drizzle,
each drop of rain lit from within.

I lie down. I'm not sure
if it's tarmac or carpet.
Someone kisses me.
I love you.
I'm out of my depth.

Somebody else kisses me, whispers,
and I go down deep.
Are they bringing me back from the dead?
I can hear voices.
Someone feeds me Baileys
from a plastic tumbler – Sophie,
her perfume filling my head,
rousing me. I rise into mist
and birdsong, I stand in the road
with my arms out wide, like Jesus.
I'm dressed in rain, silvered, incandescent.
This is the world on a Sunday morning.

A hiker walks by with his tent and walking poles
in a world of his own, I don't think
he even sees us, he's off up the coffin path,
his head full of rain and cloud.
He is not of this world any more than I.

Miranda is dancing in the circle
of the mini-roundabout, an image from long ago,
some earlier dawn.

There's Dot and Kate and Anna, legless,
talking art and poetry, the meaning of life,
and love, as if it could help them,
or any one of us. Mark holds court in the kitchen,
rolling a big one, his baritone voice booms
through the house like an avalanche:
the Brontes, Wordsworth, Blackburn Rovers,
preaching to a kitchen of lunatics.

And out in the road, in the rain and mist,
Craig with his big smile, chuckling,
unfazed by the weather, the drugs, the early morning:
portly, avuncular, the Buddha of cool.

He stands in the road at 5 a.m.
astride the white lines, chewing the root
of a joint, smiling like Clint Eastwood
at Lee Van Kleef. This is his Manor,
this kingdom of rain and madness.

Look at the light, she says rushing out
into the dawn, down the A591,
her skin aglow, through the hotel gardens
and into the lake, where she disappears like an otter,
her coat running with diamonds.

The water swallows her, the light obscures the dark
shadow of her body heading out into emerald,
the shimmering green water, and she doesn't come up.

GPS

The dark comes quickly here, like doubt,
at four the colour drains out of everything;
fog stirs on the hill and the path dissolves.

High Raise: bitch of a fell in winter,
gloomy and dank, silent, except for the tick–
ticking of moss as it drinks. You walk

by your nerves, the map redundant as you sink
into darkness and panic. Thank God
for your GPS, its ghostly glow in your hand,

for satellites hung above you, cold, angelic,
guardians to lost hikers, fools and the reckless.
They plot your route step by step.

You pray for the life of your batteries, and trust
in a science born out of war, and slaughter.
You follow blindly, letting them guide you down,

as they guide a missile down the air-con shaft
of a factory where the innocent crouch.
You move through a valley, bog after bog,

then over the lip of a ridge, stony and buckled,
walking from waypoint to waypoint,
into a gentler landscape, the sound of sheep,

a beck somewhere, crashing the stillness,
a dry stone wall, miracle of the sudden path.
The lights of a distant farm blister the darkness

and you're home, buzzing, walking on air
all the way to the pub, where you toast
your little beauty with a pint, a kiss and a prayer

to providence, to missile systems brooding in silos,
to Euclid and Newton, to the intrigues of sine,
cosine, and tangent for getting you home.

Arrival

Where has he come from,
how did he get here, through what
vast spaces has he travelled
across what skies and oceans
to get here, to this strange place,
full of light and cold?
He stands on four unsteady legs,
the white, miraculous breath
billowing out of him. He glistens
and shines in a space-suit of viscera,
electric blue, and green.
What has he seen, what knowledge
has he brought from the secret heart
of matter, this traveller
who only an hour ago surfaced
through an amniotic dreamscape
into a frosty field at the end of the lane?
Why has he come? What news
does he bring? He finds his feet
and looks at the meaningless world
like a horse-headed god in an alien land.
He stands there, steaming in frost,
victorious, like one who has journeyed far,
and found a resting place in paradise.
He clears his throat and whinnies,
and what he means we cannot know,
it could be the answer to everything,
or maybe its simply – look, I'm a horse,
the water is cold and the grass is good.

Ancestors

We all without a single exception inherit
all our genes from an unbroken line
of successful ancestors.
                      Richard Dawkins

When I reach for you in the hot night
I wonder, do I really want you,
or are my genes on fire for some distant shore?
As we fuck in the night, I can hear them singing,
choir to choir in the endless dark.
I think of our ancestors, the distance
they travelled – out of the slime
and into the trees, through all the ice ages
and the shifting of continents.
They came through plagues that wasted millions,
hunger, poverty, war. Not one of them
failed to find a mate. They slipped through aeons
passing their code from body to body,
to me and you in the distant future,
a childless couple drinking beer,
talking politics and science. To think
it all ends here for these particular passengers,
to have come this far, and found a blank. If I were
the sentimental type,
I'd take you now in the alley behind this bar,
and do the honourable thing:
I'd open the floodgates and let them go,
screaming and singing into the future.

Frog March

It's only when you've stood on one
that you notice, these mud coloured frogs,
the size of a finger nail hopping
all over Red Bank Road in the early light,
heading to meadows from spawning grounds
down by the lake, you can't help crushing them,
there are thousands braving the black macadam,
the tourist buses, tractors and mountain bikes.
They hop like miniscule, mad beserkers,
as traffic mows them down by the pond-full.

I can't be lolly-pop man to these amphibian hoards.
They're not men, with families, crossing continents,
full of stories of flight; the accumulated history
of suffering, sadness and joy: just frogs.
If enough pass over and climb the far bank
and sink into pools of clean fell-water,
then all is well. One in a thousand is all it takes.

I walk back hours later, and the road
is bound in a fine frog-skin,
brown and tacky underfoot, the faint whiff
of blood and pond weed in the cool air,
a drizzle starting, an owl hooting
in Red Bank woods, and all the traffic gone
for now. A free run at last, though god knows
something will be waiting in the grass
on the other side, licking its chops at such
an easy feast; a whole hillside of hungry
predators. It just never stops.

Fledgling

*A small bird will drop frozen dead from a bough
without ever having felt sorry for itself.*
                    D.H. Lawrence

It must have crashed on its first, ill-fated
flight, straight into the box of empty bottles
and beer cans by the back door.

There's no way home for this one now,
whose mother keeps coming to feed it still,
between the cider and the Holsten pils.

It cowers when I come to look, and hisses
if I get too close. There's nothing I can do
to save it, or save its mother's grief,

if that's what she feels. I didn't invent the birds.
I can't return it to the nest. It cocks its head
to listen to the maddening birdsong.

Soon the cats will take it apart on the lawn
while its mother sits nearby
on a fence post, shrieking in futile protest.

Tomorrow as the sun comes up,
the dawn chorus will fill the garden,
and she will sing her song again,

without hope or sadness, but full of gusto,
beautifully, from the top of the apple tree,
as she always does.

Still-life with Cricketers

for the Pomroys

Almost timeless you'd think,
the lie of these fields and valleys,
this emerald amphitheatre
carved out of grass. A game of cricket
played under the high sun; theatre
of idle dreams, tomfoolery,
batters and bowlers, dozy fielders
nursing their hangovers.
Every shade and half shade of green
shifts in sunlight and shadow.
Over the shimmer of moth-wing, wasp
and grasshopper, above the steady hiss
of insect life, a buzzard calls.
It circles, dead centre of everything,
patrolling its kingdom of hedgerow,
brambles and oak. This snapshot
of England, mid summer's day,
so calm a dog bark echoes
off three different hills.
You lift your head and catch it like this:
green on green, the white of a lake,
the blur of a cricket ball gracing the sky,
and a daytime moon, suspended like ice
in a beaker of blue gin.

Mean

from an installation
by Roy Voss

What's the message
with these
semiotic stutterings,
these idle signs
in the landscape:
Dear Dear. Come Come,
each snowy mountain
mimics itself
almost exactly,
a double take,
of snowflake, forest
and lake. There There,
here, or here; where
will it all end?
She loves me,
she loves me not,
she blows the seed
off a dandelion clock.
Ding dong. Spunk.
Nice place to sleep,
under canvas.
Camp cunt.
You can't label me.

Little Langdale
cleansed of cottages,
empty, warped:
on second thoughts
this is no place to get
it up,
the tent, dear, the tent.
What does it mean?
all this silage *(sic)*.
What is the signifier?
What's the signified?
Polite Notice:
Fuck Off.

Reply

after Catullus: Carmen 16

I'll have your fucking arses Pox and Quim:
gob-shite and bum poet. Clever little shits.
You think I mess with eggs in bed, hit
golf balls on the moon, and live in sin,

because I use first person in my verse,
or can't count stresses in a line, like you:
(that's five, and so is this, in iambs too).
Perhaps it's just the sex that makes you curse

you little runts, I wouldn't be surprised.
I don't write poems for cunts like you, who yearn
for verses dense and formalised.
I know exactly what it is that turns

you on; just spread your cheeks, you little queers,
I'll shove this dirty cock right up your rears.

Grizedale Tarn

I could not help thinking we should see him again
because he was only going to Penrith. Dorothy Wordsworth

At Grizedale Tarn I watch you turn
and walk down the path to Patterdale,
your red cagoule bright as hawthorn berries
in the autumn light. Beyond – the Vale of Eden
like a promised land, fertile, green.

It must have been right here
that William and Dorothy waved
their brother off that final time.
I wonder how long they lingered?
Did they wait until he disappeared
for good, then walk the long walk home,
in emptiness and silence?

The tarn gives nothing back, it's dark
and reticent; a solitary tent, a man fishing.
I walk back home to Grasmere, gloomy,
full of thought, your absence everywhere.

Tornado

It's here without warning, a sudden
shriek, and it's down your throat –
so low you can see the payload
slung below the wings, the pilot
nursing his joy. Too late – it's hit you–
the windows rattle their frames,
the 'Moonlight Sonata' struggles for sense
as the radio judders along the window ledge.
The sheep in the field continue
their slow munching through grass,
oblivious, they've seen it all before.
It turns with a rumble: beautiful
the way the air holds it, how it weeps
in the atmosphere, the watery vortices
trailing off wingtips; it throttles out
and is gone, a dot on the far horizon.
Immaculate. How can you not love it?
The whole valley could be ash by now
and we'd never have felt a thing.

The Bus

for Tommy

You empty your wallet and take a seat
on the 555 to Keswick, the supermarket run.
It stands at the bus stop hyperventilating in the rain,
psyching itself for the slog up Dunmail Raise.
As it headbutts its way up the pass, like a pugilist,
single minded, brutal, you look at your change,
and sigh – you could have drunk all night on that.
Wind and rain slap the windows blind,
shaking the whole body of the bus.
It doesn't come cheap, but nothing will stop
this beast of a bus as it climbs the cleavage
between Steel Fell and Great Tongue.
It's had worse batterings than this.
You can travel all the way from Blackpool
to Gateshead on the same ticket, the driver
likes to inform you, which is little comfort,
but one day you'll do that, just to spite him.
Still, it's quite a journey over the top:
the darkness of Thirlmere, the slopes of Helvellyn,
the sweep of St John in the Vale.
We're flogged by the branches of trees as we go,
plunging through floods, a blizzard of hail
stoning the bus, turning the windows white.
It's not pretty, it'll rob you blind, but whatever
the weather, you know it'll get you home.